SHOES, CHOCS, BAGS and FROCKS

for Tara

HarperCollins*Publishers*
77–85 Fulham Palace Road,
Hammersmith, London W6 8JB

www.harpercollins.co.uk

Published by HarperCollins*Publishers* 2007
5 7 9 8 6

The Author asserts the moral right to
be identified as the author of this work

A catalogue record for this book
is available from the British Library

ISBN 13 978-0-00-724757-8
ISBN 10 0-00-724757-5

Printed in China by Leo Paper

SHOES, CHOCS, BAGS and FROCKS

"Buy me, Lady," said the frock, "and I will make you into a BEAUTIFUL and WHOLE and COMPLETE Human Being."

"Do not be SILLY," said the Man, "for a frock alone cannot do that."

"TRUE," said the Lady. "I will have the Shoes and the Bag as well."

The BEAUTIFUL FROCK

MY "KILLER" HEELS

When I wear my Killer Heels, men will GASP with passion, lust and longing, and girls will SIGH with envy and despair.

For I shall be the total QUEEN of HOTNESS, and they shall be my faithful, humble SLAVES.

So powerful was their spell that ladies SIGHED with PLEASURE at their beauty and grown men fell to their knees and WEPT

The WONDERFUL UNDIES

HAIR

I don't want to be a HAIR
I want to be a DRAGON!

SHUT UP!!!

ok I'll be a hair

Observation

When all is said and done, women are very often RIGHT

Conclusion

Women must get their instructions from a HIGHER AUTHORITY than men.

For Further Research

Why is that AUTHORITY so interested in SHOPPING?

MAN vs WOMAN

A SILLY LITTLE MAN   A MAGNIFICENT WOMAN

GORGEOUS HANDBAGS

When the world seems DARK and full of SORROW,
When my feet are DRAGGING on the ground,
I simply look at all my GORGEOUS HANDBAGS
And, suddenly, TRUE HAPPINESS is found!

YOU are nearly as **LOVELY** as these.

NOTE

I hope you know just how incredibly **LOVELY** that makes you.

The LOVELINESS of YOU

SHOES

CHOCOLATE

THE PANTS OF PEACE

May they bring LOVE
and HAPPINESS to all
who wear them

When I am in charge
everyone who is LOVELY
will get a BIG HAT

That will be THE LAW!!

THE "LOVELY" HATS

MY CHOCOLATE KINGDOM

<u>a Fragment of a Dream</u>

... and in my Chocolate Kingdom they brought me great MOUNTAINS of CHOCOLATE and thereof did I eat. And it did not make me feel ILL or ASHAMED, neither did it put weight on my THIGHS. For the chocolate was health-giving and NOURISHING, and the more I ate, the more BEAUTIFUL I became.

This is a picture of the Wonderful Girl. She is beautiful and STRONG and soft all at the same time.

Everyone who meets her LOVES her and she spreads HAPPINESS wherever she goes.

She is not even frightened of SPIDERS.

THE WONDERFUL GIRL

The SHOE of SALVATION

SHOE: Look at me. Am I not wonderful?

LADY: You are the most wonderful shoe in the world. I fall to my knees and weep with pleasure when I am with you.

PAUSE

LADY: You are BEAUTY. You are TRUTH. In you I find my SALVATION.

SHOE: Thank you. You are a nice lady.

Such was the POWER of the Handbag of Glory that ladies WEPT when they saw it and those who TOUCHED it went straight to HEAVEN

The HANDBAG of GLORY

The LADY and the CHOCOLATE

LADY

CHOCOLATE

CHOCOLATE: You want me Lady don't you? You want me! YOU WANT ME!

LADY: No Chocolate, I do not want you, for after the initial pleasure there is SICKNESS and there is GUILT.

CHOCOLATE: That, Lady is the REASON FOR MY EXISTENCE. Are you to deny me the REASON FOR MY EXISTENCE?

LADY: No, chocolate. I would not do that.

CHOCOLATE: Thank you.

(A munching sound is heard, followed by a sigh of pleasure.)

THE END